P9-CMW-952

# Shrimp

by Colleen Sexton

BLASTOFF!
2
READERS

BELLWETHER MEDIA · MINNEAPOLIS, MN

Note to Librarians, Teachers, and Parents:

**Blastoff! Readers** are carefully developed by literacy experts and combine standards-based content with developmentally appropriate text.

**Level 1** provides the most support through repetition of high-frequency words, light text, predictable sentence patterns, and strong visual support.

**Level 2** offers early readers a bit more challenge through varied simple sentences, increased text load, and less repetition of high-frequency words.

**Level 3** advances early-fluent readers toward fluency through increased text and concept load, less reliance on visuals, longer sentences, and more literary language.

**Level 4** builds reading stamina by providing more text per page, increased use of punctuation, greater variation in sentence patterns, and increasingly challenging vocabulary.

**Level 5** encourages children to move from "learning to read" to "reading to learn" by providing even more text, varied writing styles, and less familiar topics.

Whichever book is right for your reader, Blastoff! Readers are the perfect books to build confidence and encourage a love of reading that will last a lifetime!

This edition first published in 2009 by Bellwether Media, Inc.

No part of this publication may be reproduced in whole or in part without written permission of the publisher. For information regarding permission, write to Bellwether Media, Inc., Attention: Permissions Department, Post Office Box 19349, Minneapolis, MN 55419.

Library of Congress Cataloging-in-Publication Data
Sexton, Colleen A., 1967–
  Shrimp / by Colleen Sexton.
    p. cm. – (Blastoff! readers. Oceans alive)
  Includes bibliographical references and index.
  Summary: "Simple text and supportive images introduce beginning readers to shrimp. Intended for students in kindergarten through third grade"–Provided by publisher.
  ISBN-13: 978-1-60014-252-9 (hardcover : alk. paper)
  ISBN-10: 1-60014-252-4 (hardcover : alk. paper)
  1. Shrimps–Juvenile literature. I. Title.

QL444.M33S49 2009
595.3'88–dc22                              2008033543

# Contents

Shrimp are **crustaceans**.
They live in oceans all over
the world.

They often live together in large groups.

Some shrimp hide near shore during the day. They come out at night to feed.

Shrimp have narrow bodies
that end in a tail.

Shrimp can be many different colors. Most shrimp are gray, brown, white, or pink.

Some are red, purple, green, or blue. Some have stripes or spots.

Some shrimp change color
to match their surroundings.
They can hide from **predators**.

Many shrimp light up. They can squirt bright clouds from their bodies to scare away predators.

Shrimp do not have bones.
A hard shell protects a
shrimp's soft body.

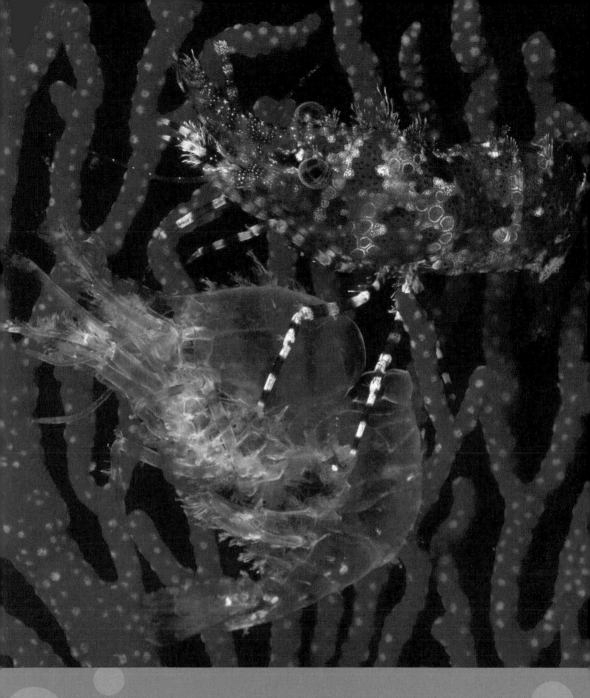

A shrimp **molts** as it grows.
The shell cracks open and
the shrimp wiggles out.

A new shell hardens over the
shrimp's body.

**stalks**

Shrimp have eyes on **stalks**.

Shrimp have jaws for eating.
They eat **plankton**, fish, and
the eggs of other ocean animals.

16

antennas

Shrimp have four long **antennas**. They use their antennas to feel, smell, and taste.

17

walking legs

Shrimp have ten walking legs near the front of their bodies.

claws

Some shrimp have **claws** on their front legs. They use their claws to dig, fight, and gather food.

swimming legs

Shrimp have ten swimming legs shaped like paddles. Shrimp swim forward most of the time.

Shrimp can change direction to escape danger. Swish! They flip their tails and swim backward.

# Glossary

**antennas**—feelers on an animal's head used to touch, taste, and smell

**claw**—a hard, curved nail at the end of an animal's leg

**crustaceans**—a group of animals that have a hard outer shell, legs with joints, and a body divided into parts; crabs, lobsters, crayfish, and shrimp are all crustaceans.

**molt**—to lose the hard outer shell so that a new, bigger shell can grow

**plankton**—tiny living things that float in the ocean and are food for other animals; plankton are too small to be seen with the human eye.

**predator**—an animal that hunts other animals for food; shrimp are food for many ocean animals.

**stalk**—a thin part that connects one thing to another; a stalk connects a shrimp's eyes to its body.

# To Learn More

## AT THE LIBRARY

Sill, Cathryn. *About Crustaceans: A Guide for Children*. Atlanta, Ga.: Peachtree, 2004.

Stone, Lynn M. *Shrimp*. Vero Beach, Fla.: Rourke, 2003.

Tate, Suzanne. *Sammy Shrimp: A Tale of a Little Shrimp*. Nags Head, N.C.: Nags Head Art, 1990.

## ON THE WEB

Learning more about shrimp is as easy as 1, 2, 3.

1. Go to www.factsurfer.com.

2. Enter "shrimp" into the search box.

3. Click the "Surf" button and you will see a list of related Web sites.

With factsurfer.com, finding more information is just a click away.

# Index

The images in this book are reproduced through the courtesy of: Nikita Tiunov, front cover, p. 7; Lisa Turay, p. 4; JUNIORS BILDARCHIV / age fotostock, p. 5; Norbert Wu / Getty Images, pp. 6, 20; Jeff Hunter, p. 8; James D. Watt / Image Quest 3-D, p. 9; Brandon Cole, p. 10; Jeff Rotman / Alamy, p. 11; Jez Tryner / Image Quest Marine, pp. 12-13, 15; Mark Aplet, p. 14; E.R. Degginger / Alamy, pp. 16-17; Visual & Written SL / Alamy, p. 18; David Fleetham / Alamy, p. 19; Getty Images, p. 21.